SHERLOCK PUZZ

Sherlock Puzzle Book (Volume 4)

Unsolved Mysteries and Cases Documented by Dr. John Watson

Mildred T. Walker

SHERLOCK PUZZLE BOOK (VOLUME 4)

SHERLOCK PUZZLE BOOK (VOLUME 4)

purposes only. All effort has been executed to present accurate, up to date, reliable, complete information. No warranties of any kind are declared or implied. Readers acknowledge that the author is not engaged in the rendering of legal, financial, medical or professional advice. The content within this book has been derived from various sources. Please consult a licensed professional before attempting any techniques outlined in this book.

By reading this document, the reader agrees that under no circumstances is the author responsible for any losses, direct or indirect, that are incurred as a result of the use of the information contained within this document, including, but not limited to, errors, omissions, or inaccuracies.

Bluesource And Friends

This book is brought to you by Bluesource And Friends, a happy book publishing company.

Our motto is **"Happiness Within Pages"**

We promise to deliver amazing value to readers with our books.

We also appreciate honest book reviews from our readers.

Connect with us on our Facebook page www.facebook.com/bluesourceandfriends and stay tuned to our latest book promotions and free giveaways.

Don't forget to claim your FREE books!

Brain Teasers:

https://tinyurl.com/karenbrainteasers

Harry Potter Trivia:
https://tinyurl.com/wizardworldtrivia

Also check out our other books

"67 Lateral Thinking Puzzles"

https://tinyurl.com/thinkingandriddles

"Rookstorm Online Saga"

https://tinyurl.com/rookstorm

"Korman's Prayer"

https://tinyurl.com/kormanprayer

"The Convergence"

https://tinyurl.com/bloodcavefiction

"The Hardest Sudokos In Existence (Ranked As The Hardest Sudoku Collection Available In The Western World)"

https://tinyurl.com/MasakiSudoku

SHERLOCK PUZZLE BOOK (VOLUME 4)

Table of Contents

SHERLOCK PUZZLE BOOK (VOLUME 4)

SHERLOCK PUZZLE BOOK (VOLUME 4)

SHERLOCK PUZZLE BOOK (VOLUME 4)

19th August 1889

I would like to state how fortunate I am to witness the absolute brilliance that is Sherlock Holmes. I work with him on many occasions and offer my medical opinion and advice on some of his cases, although I don't think he actually requires my assistance that much. Being able to watch him work on a day-to-day basis is an incredible privilege.

I have lived with Sherlock Holmes at 221B Baker Street for many years, and I believe that time has been incredibly enriching for both me and Sherlock. My name is John Watson, and I am a doctor.

Throughout the years of working with Sherlock and joining him on his cases, I have had multiple opportunities to improve my way of thinking. It was Sherlock himself that provided me with these opportunities. He would often see a riddle or an enigma, the answer of which would be very clear to him, and ask my opinion on the matter. He would already know the answer, but would push me to find it myself. I think this has improved my mind and the way I see the world. Sherlock has enriched my life in so many ways through this method of his.

SHERLOCK PUZZLE BOOK (VOLUME 4)

I believe that his methods are a bit strange, but they do bear results. I am quicker on my feet now than I was in my youth. I see answers where others would fail to look for them, and I am capable of solving various puzzles in a matter of time. I owe my new-found knowledge and experiences all to my friend and colleague, without whom I would still be puzzled by the simplest of riddles.

Sherlock Holmes, in my opinion, has the greatest mind in our age. He sees things in a way that no one else ever will. I'm sure you've heard of him at some point. His name and achievements have been consistently splattered all over front pages of newspapers. He is quite the detective. My skills can come nowhere near his, but I will try my best while working on this book.

My friend and dear colleague has always wanted to spread his gift of knowledge. He has wanted to bring his method of thinking to the world. He spoke often of his desire to compile a collection of his knowledge and cases into one book. He said he wanted the world to read it and be compelled to think as he does. To put all of his knowledge and experiences into one book would be an achievement unto itself, but I have done my best to compile all the knowledge I have gained over the many years working by his side.

SHERLOCK PUZZLE BOOK (VOLUME 4)

For those who read this book that also find themselves struggling with simple questions and riddles, I can promise that this will help. These are the exact same exercises that Sherlock gave me in order to help my way of thinking and the speed at which I can solve cases. Sherlock found these riddles, puzzles, and enigmas to be child's play and simple, whereas I found them difficult and complex. You will probably see them the same way, but don't worry. I learned to overcome my old way of thinking and see the puzzles from a new angle. When you learn to do this, the answer actually becomes quite clear and simple.

Read on and discover the knowledge I have gathered over the years. Help Sherlock and I solve these cases and gain an eagle's-eye view into the mind of the world's greatest detective. If you get stuck, do not worry - the answers for each case can be found at the end of this book. These answers are either conclusions I had come to myself or explanations given to me by Mr. Holmes. Do not feel daunted by the realization that you may miss a case or not fully understand the answer to each riddle. When you open your mind and see things the way a detective would, you will feel your mind grow stronger with each task given to you.

SHERLOCK PUZZLE BOOK (VOLUME 4)

I will be glad if this book helps improve your way of thinking and sharpen your mind. The credit cannot go to me solely, for these are Sherlock's cases and this is his way of life. I am merely along for the journey. However, if you find that this does not help you to improve your thinking, please blame me and not my friend. I have done my best to convey his thoughts and answers, but I accept your judgment if I have failed in doing so.

Now dear friends, allow me to present a collection of the unsolved cases of Sherlock Holmes.

Dr. John Watson

The Case of the Murdered Architect

When Mr. Holmes and I first arrived at the circular mansion, we were both shocked and amused by the building's structure. It was a perfectly round building. The owner of the building was Mr. Arch Digger, an award-winning architect. He was found dead by his desk in the early hours of January eighth. The police were quite confused by the circumstances of his death, so they called in Sherlock Holmes, the greatest detective in England, for some assistance.

We arrived to find several members of the household lined up outside, surrounded by police officers. I followed Sherlock as he walked up to the officer-in-charge at the scene.

"What seems to be the problem, Officer?" Sherlock asked.

"The owner of the household, Mr. Arch Digger, was murdered this morning. These members of the household were all within the home at the time of the murder. We suspect one of them to be guilty. The problem is, they all have alibis."

"I see," Sherlock studied the line of suspects. "Do you mind if I ask the suspects a few questions?"

"Not at all, Mr. Holmes."

I stayed quiet and followed closely behind Sherlock as he walked from each suspect, asking them only one question:

"What were you doing at the time of Mr. Arch Digger's death?"

"I was busy preparing Mr. Digger's breakfast. He likes having eggs and sausages in the morning." The cook replied.

"I was attending to the house, cleaning the shelves, dusting the books, and sweeping the corners as usual." The maid responded.

"I was still asleep, I'm afraid. I drank a little too much last night, you see." Mrs. Digger explained.

"I was in the garden of course! That's what gardeners do!" The gardener rudely pointed out.

Sherlock stood back and thought for a moment. He looked at me.

"What do you think, Watson?" He asked.

I looked shocked, of course, I wasn't expecting him to ask me for my opinion on the matter.

"I'm not sure I understand," I replied.

"Well, one of these four people is the murderer, Watson. The clues are right in front of us and practically quite obvious. They basically said 'I'm the murderer' with their statement. Who do you think it is?"

I thought for a moment and ran all of the suspects statements through my head for a second time. In the end, it was actually quite obvious.

Who murdered the architect?

The Case of the Vanishing Bank Robber

The Bank of England was robbed during the cold months. Mr. Holmes and I were fortunate enough to be in the area, so we decided to lend our expertise to the officers at the scene. Sherlock was very intrigued by the incident.

We walked into the nearby park and watched the police officers search the area. A group of them were gathered around the lake at the center of the park. The lake's surface was frozen over, except for one man-sized hole near the edge of it.

"What seems to be the problem, officers?" Sherlock asked the gathered policemen.

"Uh! Mr. Holmes, thank goodness you're here. The bank robber has disappeared!"

"Is that so?" Sherlock scanned the area and spotted a pile of wet clothes near the hole in the frozen lake. "I believe the bank robber is still in the park and hiding nearby."

"How could you possibly know that?" The officers were quite taken aback by Sherlock's conclusion, as was I.

He smiled and looked back at me.

"Dear Watson, would you care to explain to these officers why I believe the bank robber to be hiding nearby?"

"Me? Mr. Holmes, I'm not sure I'm up for the task." I responded.

"It's elementary, my dear Watson. All you have to do is look at the evidence before us and think outside the box."

I did as Mr. Holmes suggested, and in the end the answer was staring me right in the face.

What happened to the bank robber?

The Case of the Slow Drinker

Mr. Holmes and I were having a spot of tea one early morning when the phone rang. I, of course, got up to answer it.

"It's Scotland Yard, Sherlock. They've asked if you could go down there at once." I informed him.

Sherlock put his teacup down and we left for Scotland Yard immediately. When we got there, the police officer led us to the morgue, where a dead man's body lay on the table.

"Why am I here, Officer?" Sherlock asked, completely unimpressed with the situation.

"This man is dead," the officer responded.

"Yes, I can see that. Why does that involve me?"

"We don't know how he died. He was down at the pub with his friend and they were both drinking some whiskey. Then, he just dropped dead."

"How many glasses of whiskey did he have?" I asked the officer.

"Only one, Doctor, and his friend had about six glasses, himself." The officer responded.

"That is strange - so he didn't die from alcohol poisoning."

"Perhaps he died from actual poisoning." Sherlock suggested. "Maybe someone put some poison in his glass?"

"Him and his friend ordered a bottle of whiskey and they were drinking from the same bottle. If the bottle was poisoned, then they would both be dead." The police officer corrected him.

"This is quite the enigma, Watson, I wonder what could have killed him." Sherlock stood there and thought for a moment.

"Should I do an autopsy?" I suggested. "Then I may find whatever it is that killed the poor fellow."

Sherlock shook his head, "No, I don't think that will be necessary." He turned to the police officer. "When you found the man's dead body, was he at the pub?" The officer nodded. "Was there ice in any of the two men's glasses?"

The officer thought for a moment, "Yes, there was ice in both their glasses."

"That's it, then," Sherlock smiled to himself. "This man was indeed poisoned."

"Mr. Holmes, how on Earth can you be certain of that?" I asked.

"It's quite simple, Watson."

How was the man poisoned?

The Case of the Dead Man in the Snow

The cold months of winter are the worst for me and Sherlock, but a good mystery always manages to cheer him up. We were called out to the woods, late in the afternoon, to assist the police with a dead man they found in the snow.

I stood back with the police officers and watched Sherlock examine the scene of the crime - if there was a crime. There seemed to be no evidence in the area, but Sherlock had found something that no one else could.

"Watson! Won't you come over here for a moment?" Sherlock called to me and I made my way over to him. "I think I have solved it. However, I thought I'd give you a go at figuring it out for yourself."

"I'm not sure I'll be able to, Mr. Holmes, but I'll give it a try."

I examined the scene and found what appeared to be nothing at all. There was a set of footprints leading towards the dead mans' body. The footprints matched those of the dead man. There were no other footprints in the area, no murder weapon, no blood, and the only other markings in the snow were two parallel lines leading up to the body, or away from it.

I examined the lines. They were deep in the snow, but I couldn't yet tell what they were from. The lines were on the outside of the dead man's footprints and they had not disturbed them. Therefore, the lines were not made by something large being dragged from the body. The parallel lines must have been made by two thin objects, wide enough to go around the trail of footprints.

"I've got it!" I exclaimed as the answer popped into my head.

"I knew you could do it, dear Watson. You just need to think outside the box."

"Who is the murderer then?" One of the police officers asked us.

Who should the police be looking for?

The Case of the Missing Mail

Sherlock and I made our way to the scene of the crime on a Thursday morning after being called down there by the head inspectors at Scotland Yard. We were told nothing of the case at hand, only that they had found a dead body and they weren't sure what to do next.

We walked into the house of the victim to find the dead body lying on the floor in a puddle of blood. The officers were gathered outside the house and let us straight in. I examined the crime scene with Sherlock and pointed out all the evidence I could find to him.

"The puddle of blood is dry and soaked into the wooden floor," I explained. "That means the body has been here for at least a few days."

"I would have guessed that from the smell," the inspector said as he interrupted us. "Here's what we know. The mailman came to drop off her mail this morning and that's when he found her. He said when he passed the door, he smelt something awful inside, and so he glanced through the letter box to see her body lying on the floor. Other than that, there is no evidence. No weapon, point of entry, or fingerprints. What do you think, Mr. Holmes?"

My eyes fell on Sherlock as he continued to study the crime scene. He examined the stack of papers near the door and studied them closely. He then stood up, turned to me, and said:

"The mailman is your murderer!"

How did he know the mailman did it?

The Case of the Two Wives

I was sitting at the table reading this morning's newspaper while Sherlock was at his desk tinkering with some evidence from a cold case he found. There was a knock on the door and the landlord walked in.

"You have a client, Mr. Holmes," the landlord informed us.

"Thank goodness for that; I was beginning to grow bored," Sherlock sighed as he stood from his desk. "Send them in, please."

I stood up and joined Sherlock's side as we waited for our client to enter the room. To our shock and amazement, Benny Harley, an extremely wealthy businessman, walked in.

"Good day, Mr. Holmes. I've heard a lot about you and I require your brilliant detective skills," Benny Harley stated. "You see, I was in a rather nasty accident that sent me into a coma. I woke up quite unharmed; however, I seemed to have lost most of my memory. The doctors said it was temporary amnesia and that I should regain my original memory soon."

"I see," Sherlock nodded his head. "How can I assist you?"

"The problem is my wife, you see," Benny Harley continued, "or rather, both my wives. When I woke up from the coma, I was confronted by two women. Both claim to be my wife, and I'm not quite sure which one to believe."

"Why would a woman falsely claim to be your wife?" I asked.

"Probably something to do with the large amount of money I'm told I possess. In any case, I'm not sure if either of them are my wife, but I was wearing a wedding ring during the accident."

"Would you like me to investigate the women and find out which one is actually your wife?" Sherlock asked him.

"Yes, that's exactly what I want you to do. I have a picture of each of them for you to use." He dug into his coat pocket and pulled out two photos.

Sherlock and I examined the photos together. One woman was wearing a tight red dress and wore a lot of gold jewelry. The other woman wore a plain ring and a necklace and was dressed in a plain skirt and shirt.

"This woman is your wife," Sherlock stated almost instantly and handed the picture of the woman dressed in a plain skirt and shirt back to the man.

"How did you know?"

"Yes, Sherlock, how did you know?" I asked him.

How did he know which woman was the man's wife?

The Case of the Coded Kidnapper

There was a kidnapping at 234 Baker Street and Sherlock and I were appointed to the case. We arrived promptly to speak with the Scotland Yard inspectors to view the evidence as well as the crime scene.

"The man who was kidnapped was Mr. Harold Green," the inspector explained. "All we have to go on are three suspects who had motive for the kidnapping and a strange note left behind by the victim himself." The inspector handed Sherlock the note. "We suspect that he knew the person who kidnapped him and he was trying to leave behind a warning without alerting the kidnapper. What do you make of it, Mr. Holmes?"

Sherlock studied the note and I leaned in to give it a look myself. The note read:

His name can be found in;

The first of January

The fourth of October

The fifth of March

The third of June

"Interesting," Sherlock hummed as he put the note down. "Who are your suspects?"

"Jennifer Green, the daughter and heir to her father's property; Jules Green, Mr. Harold's wife; and John Blacksmith, the bodyguard to the Green family. They each have a motive."

"I don't need to hear the motives, inspector, I'm sure the name of the kidnapper can be found in this note, if we can decipher it." Sherlock handed the note to me. "What do you think, Watson?"

I took the note from Sherlock and read it again and again until something clicked inside my brain and I knew who the kidnapper was.

Who is the kidnapper?

The Case of the Unfortunate Camping Trip

Mr. Holmes and I waited outside of Scotland Yard for the inspector. He called us down here for some help identifying a murderer. It's been so quiet lately that Sherlock was positively excited about the situation. He was keen to give his mind a bit of an exercise. I was sure he would try to get my brain thinking as well.

The inspector came to get us and led us to the interrogation room. Inside the room were two men. One man was wearing a suit and tie with perfectly combed hair. The other man was wearing a pair of jeans and a clean shirt with uncombed hair.

Sherlock studied them for a moment and then turned to the inspector.

"What would you like my help with this time, inspector?"

"These two men were the last to see our murder victim, Tim Brook," the inspector explained. "Mr. Brook was found dead in the woods yesterday. Seven days ago, Tim and his friend Alex, the man with the uncombed hair, went camping out in the woods. The only person they informed of their trip was Steven Brook, Tim's brother, the man with the combed hair."

"You suspect either Steven Brook or Alex are responsible for murdering Tim Brook?" I asked the inspector.

"They were the only two who knew about the trip. However, Steven Brook insists that he has been held up at his work for the past seven days and that he has not seen his brother since they left for the camping trip. Alex, the man who went with him, states that he got lost in the woods the first night they arrived and has been wandering through the woods for the past seven days." The inspector sighed and shook his head. "Unfortunately, we have no idea which one of them is telling the truth and which one of them murdered Tim Brook. That's where you come in, Mr. Holmes. Can you identify the killer?"

Sherlock peered into the interrogation room and studied each man closely. I had a feeling he was taking his time and enjoying the exercise. He eventually turned to me and smiled knowingly.

"Watson, would you like to have the honor of solving this one?" He asked me. "It's actually quite a simple case if you look at the evidence the right way."

"What evidence is that, exactly?" I asked as I joined Sherlock by his side.

"The evidence is right in front of you, dear Watson."

I studied the suspects as Sherlock had done and after a short while I spotted the evidence that Sherlock had spotted earlier. I knew who the killer was.

Who is the killer?

The Case of the Strange Note

Sherlock has many fans and sometimes we have to deal with those fans. One fan in particular loves to commit crimes and then leave notes at the scene for Sherlock. By deciphering these notes, Sherlock is able to identify the criminal. We stood at the scene of one of these exact incidents this morning and I watched Sherlock study the note left behind by the criminal just for him.

Sherlock was puzzled. I could see it on his face. It's not often that he gets confused and he usually doesn't stay that way for very long.

"Watson, I have it!" Sherlock cried out and turned to me with an excited smile on his face. "I have deciphered the note and I know who our criminal is."

"I wouldn't go as far as to call him a criminal," I told Sherlock. "His crime isn't exactly one of legend."

"He threw a stone through my window last night and it almost hit me on the head," Sherlock complained, "and he has the guts to leave this note behind for me, so that I can track him down."

"What does the note say?"

Sherlock handed me the note and I studied it carefully. It read;

"? Hollow. He threw the stone through your window. ? Hollow."

"This is a strange note indeed," I stated, "but you said you've already solved it."

"Yes I have, Watson. The answer was actually quite obvious since it is written in plain text right in front of you."

Who broke Sherlock's window?

The Case of the Missing Hiker

Aleister Bartley is a rich businessman and a thrill seeker. A month ago, he booked a trip out of the country for himself and his business partner. They were both hikers and they decided to go climb the mountains and hiking trails in Japan. A month later, only Aleister Bartley returned from the trip and he told police that his friend had an unfortunate accident and went missing in the mountains in Japan. Nobody could find him.

I read this story in the newspaper and told Mr. Holmes about it. He was intrigued by the story, but something didn't seem quite right to him.

"What travel agency did they use to book the tickets? Do you have their number?" Sherlock asked me.

I searched the name given in the newspaper and found the number of the travel agency. I gave it to Sherlock and he called them. He spoke on the phone with them briefly, explaining that he is a detective and he wants some information about the trip that Aleister Bartley booked to Japan. I waited patiently until the end of the phone call.

Sherlock hung up the phone and turned to me.

"We must make our way to Scotland Yard at once!" He stated and fetched his jacket. "We must inform them that Aleister Barley is a guilty man and that his business partner was murdered."

"How could you possibly know that?"

"It's elementary, my dear Watson."

How did Sherlock know Aleister Bartley was a murderer?

The Case of the Sand Smuggler

The inspector recently asked for Mr. Holmes and I to go down to the border. They needed our help on a special case. Sherlock wasn't interested at first, but I insisted that he go. When we got there, the inspector led us to a small room where they were holding the suspect.

"What seems to be the problem this time, Inspector?" Sherlock asked.

"It seems like a simple case, but it's baffled my officers and many of my best detectives," the inspector explained. "The man inside this room is a known smuggler. For weeks now, we've received tips from one of our undercover officers that he is planning on smuggling something big through the border. He's ridden through the border several times on his motorcycle. All he carries with him are two full bags of sand."

"Interesting," Sherlock hummed. "He smuggles sand; how does this involve me?"

"He isn't smuggling sand, Mr. Holmes. We've been informed that he is smuggling drugs of some kind.

Each time he comes to the border, he is stopped and each time, the bags he's carrying are searched. Every single time, the test results are negative. He is simply carrying bags of sand. We know he's smuggling something across, but we just don't know what. Please, Mr. Holmes, can you help us?"

I watched Sherlock's face and I could see the cogs turning, but I could also see that he wasn't interested in the case. It wasn't interesting enough for him. I found the case extremely intriguing.

"I could take a shot at solving it if you want, Sherlock?" I suggested.

"Go ahead, Watson. I'm sure you'll find it more amusing than I."

I ran the case through my head one more time just as the inspector had told it to us. The man is a known smuggler who is smuggling something across the border. Each day, he rides his motorcycle across the border carrying only two bags of sand. Nothing is found in the bags, but they know that he is smuggling something across.

A light bulb clicked inside my head as I realized what the answer was.

"I've solved it!"

How is the smuggler doing it?

The Case of the Murder in Disguise

Mr. Holmes and I decided to go for a brief walk through the nearby park on a lovely summer day. During our walk, Sherlock spotted a collection of police officers and some police tape around a house. He was excited for a bit of crime solving, and rushed over to see what was happening.

"Inspector, what is going on here?" Sherlock asked as he arrived at the crime scene.

"Mr. Holmes, I didn't expect to see you here," the inspector nodded a greeting to both I and Sherlock. "I'm afraid your services are not needed on this one. It's an open and shut case."

"Is that so? Mind if I have a look anyway?"

"Not at all," the inspector waved at the officers to let us in.

Sherlock and I walked through the house towards the crime scene. The dead body of the owner of the house was slumped in a chair by his desk with a gun on the floor beside him. Sherlock spotted a cassette recorder on the desk.

"Have you listened to this yet?" Sherlock asked the inspector.

"No we haven't. There's no need to, this is obviously a suicide."

Sherlock pressed play on the cassette recorder and the voice of the dead man came through the speakers.

"I am a sinner and so I must die as sinners do. I offer my soul to God and ask his forgiveness." The tape went silent for a moment and then there was a gunshot.

"Even more evidence to prove that it was a suicide!" The inspector pointed out. "What more do we need? He even left a suicide note."

"Actually, if anything Inspector, this suicide note proves it to be a murder." Sherlock stated with a smile.

"How do you figure that?" The inspector yelled at him.

How does Sherlock know that this is a murder in disguise?

The Case of the Guilty Husband

Mr. Holmes once told me a story of how he captured a killer while waiting to see his doctor at the hospital. He had been feeling sick and went to visit his doctor at the hospital. While he was in the waiting room, a man ran in, panicked.

"Help!" he cried out, "someone shot my wife!"

Sherlock got up straight away and went to the man to see what was going on.

"Hello, I'm detective Sherlock Holmes. Can you explain to me exactly what has happened to your wife?"

The man turned to Sherlock, a bit shocked, and told him everything.

"I was on my way home from work when I got a phone call from my housekeeper. She told me that something terrible had happened to my wife and she was sent to intensive care. I hung the phone up immediately and headed straight here."

"Is that exactly what your housekeeper told you?" Sherlock asked, reaching for the phone on the reception desk.

"Yes, those are her exact words. Now I demand to see my wife! Is she going to be okay?"

"I'm sure she's going to be okay but you're going to jail," Sherlock dialed Scotland Yard and the inspector answered. "Hello, Inspector, I need you to come down to the hospital immediately and arrest this man on suspicion of attempted murder."

"Hang on just a minute!" The man tried to back away but the security guards apprehended him. "How on Earth did you know?"

How did Sherlock know the man tried to murder his wife?

The Case of the Murdering Sons

Mr. Holmes and I were called out to the countryside to help the inspector solve a strange case of he said / she said. In this case, it was two brothers accusing the third brother of murdering their father. The inspector didn't know who to believe and so he asked us for help.

Sherlock walked ahead of me and asked all the questions while I examined the body.

The man was shot in the forehead and his body was lying at the base of the stairs in a puddle of blood. The gun was thrown to the ground near him. He was dressed in very smart attire, as if he had just arrived from a ball of some kind.

The three brothers, Jack, John, and James stood in a line beside him. The two older brothers were dressed as smartly as their father and the younger brother was dressed in casual jeans and a plain shirt. Sherlock began questioning them;

"What happened here?"

"Me, John, and our father spent most of the evening at a charity ball for the orphans," Jack explained. "Our father was a very rich and powerful man, so he liked to go to charity balls to show off his wealth by throwing it away."

"We arrived home only an hour ago," John continued. "My father had begun walking up the stairs to go to his bed when our brother James ran in through the front door and shot him."

"It was James that killed our father," Jack confirmed. "Please arrest him so that he can be punished for his crime!"

Sherlock turned to James, "Is this true?"

James shook his head and tears welled up in his eyes. "It's not true! I arrived home from a friend's house after my brothers and my father returned from the ball, but my father was already lying dead on the floor when I walked through the door."

Sherlock seemed lost in thought and quite puzzled, but I am happy to say that I had already figured out which of the brothers were lying.

Who is lying?

The Case of the Serial Killer

I arrived at 221B Baker Street after my holiday to find Mr. Holmes sitting at his desk surrounded by piles of newspapers. He was deep in reading one of them when I interrupted him.

"Sherlock, what on Earth are you up to now?"

"Watson, are you back from your holiday already?" Sherlock put the newspaper down and got up to greet me. "I am trying to solve a case. There is a serial killer on the loose and the circumstance in which he kills his victims is really quite strange."

"Are you trying to capture him?"

"No, of course not, he's not even in this country. I'm merely studying his cases to find out how he manages to kill his victims every time." Sherlock sat back down and picked up one of the newspapers. "The serial killer kidnaps his victims and then he gives them the choice of two pills. One pill is poisonous and the other is fine. The victim chooses one pill and the killer takes the second and then they both drink the pills with a glass of water."

"What is so strange about that?"

"The strange part is how the killer manages to get the safe pill every time. The two pills look identical and yet somehow the victim chooses the poisonous one each time and the killer is safe. How does he do it?"

How does the Serial Killer do it?

The Case of the Stolen Bracelet

While on vacation, Mr. Holmes got called to the police station in Paris. He had never been there before, but they had heard tales of how brilliant a detective he was and they needed his help.

"What seems to be the problem?" Sherlock asked them. "I am currently on vacation so I would ask we make this quick."

"Certainly, Mr. Holmes," the lead investigator on the case spoke. "We're sorry to bother you on your vacation, but we've heard many stories and we know that you are a great detective. We're having a problem solving this one and I know you're the man for the job."

"Okay, I'll do my best."

"A woman named Catherine came in earlier claiming that her diamond bracelet was stolen from her home while she was away. She opened up a case." The investigator gave Sherlock the photos from the scene of the crime. "We examined the crime scene and we couldn't find any evidence leading to the thief. I wonder if you will see something we didn't."

Sherlock examined the photos. The window to Catherine's bedroom was broken and there were muddy footsteps leading from the window to the dresser where she keeps her bracelet. The rest of the room was untouched and clean. Beneath the window, Sherlock saw only muddy footprints and nothing else.

He put the photos down and turned to the investigator. "I suggest you arrest Catherine on suspicion of fraud."

"What! Why?"

"She is the one who stole her own bracelet in order to claim the insurance."

How did Sherlock know?

The Case of the Prison Escape

When Sherlock returned from his vacation in Paris, he had many stories to tell me. He insisted that the trip helped him clear his head and that he felt sharper and smarter than ever.

"Sherlock, would you care to play a game?" I asked him. "I want to test you to see if your vacation has actually sharpened your skills."

"Go ahead, Watson! I'm up for the challenge."

"There is a man who has been accused of committing a crime; the crime is not important. The man has been put inside a holding cell until the police can come get him. The holding cell has no seats, a dirt floor, and an open window. The man can fit through the window but it is too high for him to reach and there is nothing to stand on. There is a shovel outside of the cell that he can reach, but he can't dig his way out of it because just below the dirt floor is a layer of thick rock." I paused to allow time for the riddle's information to sink in. "When the police arrive in the morning, the man is gone. How did he escape his cell?"

Sherlock leaned back in his chair and began to think.

How did the man escape?

The Case of the Empty Room

The room was empty except for the woman's dead body hanging from the high ceiling. I remember that case very well. It was a strange case and a very difficult one for Sherlock and I to solve.

The police were convinced it was a murder, but all the evidence stated otherwise. Sherlock and I examined the crime scene together.

The doors and windows were closed and locked from the inside. The police had to break the door down to enter. The room was completely empty. There was nothing for the woman to climb on and she had been hung by the neck from the very tall ceiling.

I examined her body. Her neck was bruised and broken so it must have been the hang from the rope that killed her. However, the woman was so short that she couldn't have climbed up to the ceiling, tied the rope to the fan, and hung herself without standing on top of something.

As mentioned before, the room was empty so there was nothing for the woman to climb onto. This is what convinced the police it was a murder. After examining the crime scene, he found a dark damp spot on the floor beneath the women. Sherlock insisted it was a suicide.

How does he know?

The Case of the Fly in his Tea

Mr. Holmes and I were due in court to testify on the behalf of Scotland Yard on a case we had helped them solve. Our train was running late so we went across the way to a small café for a cup of tea to help pass the time. It was a small café and it wasn't very clean or organized. We ordered our tea and waited ten minutes for it; thankfully our train still hadn't arrived yet.

When our cups arrived, Sherlock poured the tea for us both. I touched my mug and it was hot enough to burn my fingertips.

"Ouch!" I whispered as I pulled my hand back.

"Watch out there, Watson." Sherlock giggled at me.

I smiled at him and then looked down at my tea. Just before I reached for the sugar, I saw a fly floating at the top of my cup.

"Excuse me, Miss!" I called for the waitress and she rushed back to the table. "There's a fly in my tea, could I get a fresh cup?"

"Oh, dear! Sorry about that. I'll get you a new cup right away."

The waitress took my cup and went straight to the kitchen with it. Thankfully, I only had to wait a few moments before she returned with a new one.

"Thank you," I said as I reached for the teapot to pour myself some more tea.

Sherlock leaned over the table and picked up my mug. He examined it for a moment and gave it back to the waitress.

"This is not a new cup, it is just the last one emptied out and rinsed with some water." He told her. "Please bring my friend a new cup this time."

The waitress looked shocked and a bit embarrassed as well.

"How did you know?"

How did Sherlock know it was the same cup?

The Case of the Full House

The ride to the crime scene was slow and irritable because of the heavy traffic. Sherlock tapped his foot against the floor softly to silently demonstrate how annoyed he was. I sat back and read my newspaper, trying hard to ignore his tapping foot.

"Should I give you details of the case while we're waiting for this traffic to clear?" The inspector asked us from the front seat. "Sergeant Harry and I were there a few moments ago and we can run you through what we know so far to pass the time."

Sergeant Harry, our driver, smiled at us through the rearview mirror.

"If you must," Sherlock sighed. "At least it will get my mind off how boring this drive is. I need constant mental exercises to stay sharp."

"We have one dead victim and five suspects. The victim is Mary and she was found dead by her fiancé Bill. Bill and Mary live in a shared house with four of their friends and all of them were home at the time."

"I'm guessing they all have alibis?" I asked the inspector.

"Yes! Mike claims that he was in the kitchen cooking dinner and he had come home two hours prior to Bill finding Mary dead."

"Jack said he was out in the garden reading a book and that he had been out there all day."

"Jane is an artist and she was painting in her room all day after waking up late."

"Finally, Jenny stated that she was swimming in the pool outside for the past three hours before Mary was found and that she had the glasses of wine to prove it."

"Well let's get to the scene and see for ourselves which one of them is guilty." Sherlock said.

The traffic cleared a few minutes later and we rushed to the scene. The inspector told us that the body was found half an hour after the murder and he only spent another half an hour fetching us from 221B Baker Street.

"So an hour has passed since the murder," Sherlock mumbled. "If there is any evidence, it should still be present."

SHERLOCK PUZZLE BOOK (VOLUME 4)

Sherlock studied the suspects as they sat in the living room under guard by the police officers. He looked at them closely. Their hands were all clean and undamaged, except for Jane's hands. They were covered in paint. Jack's hands were slightly tanned, probably from reading out in the sun all day.

"I know which one of them is the murderer." Sherlock stated confidently.

Who is the murderer?

The Case of the Suspicious Death

The crime scene was laid out in front of us and it was very messy. The broken bottle of red wine soaked into the red carpet alongside the pool of blood. I examined the body of the victim while Sherlock walked around the house and examined the scene.

The husband arrived home late last night to find that his wife had shot herself in the head with his gun after having a few drinks of wine. The inspector thought that it was a suspicious death, so he called Mr. Holmes and me down to have a look ourselves.

"Where do you keep your gun?" Sherlock asked the husband.

"In a gun safe in my study upstairs," he replied.

"I assume you keep it locked when you aren't using the gun?"

"Of course!" he was quick to answer and looked offended by the question.

"I see," Sherlock left the room and went to the husband's study.

He examined the gun safe. It was empty and the safe had been opened normally using a key; it wasn't forced or broken open. He looked around the room and saw no more evidence. He returned to the crime scene and examined the dead body for a second time.

The inspector and I watched him intently as he thought carefully.

"Inspector, arrest the husband," Sherlock finally instructed. "This is clearly a murder not a suicide."

How did he know it was a murder?

The Case of the Closed Windows

A man had jumped from a building and killed himself. It was such a big story that Sherlock and I heard about it on our way back to Baker Street after a day out walking. Sherlock insisted we head over to the scene and have a look. I didn't see the point, since the man had jumped from the building, but I usually indulge Sherlock and his obsessions.

We made it to the scene. The man was splayed out on the pavement and the police were surrounding the area. The inspector let us through.

"What are you doing here, Mr. Holmes?" The inspector asked. "This is an open and shut case. There clearly isn't any need for your specialties at this time."

"Do you mind if I examine the body?" I asked.

"Not at all, Dr. Watson, though I can't imagine what you hope to find."

I like to exercise my skills just like Sherlock does, which is why I asked to examine the body.

"What can you tell me, Watson?" Sherlock asked while I was examining the body. "Can you tell how far the man fell?"

I did my best to answer his questions, "The pavement isn't damaged and most of his major bones and organs are unharmed. I would say he fell from a far height but not from the top of the building."

"That rules out the roof and the top floors." Sherlock mumbled to himself. "I'll be right back."

Sherlock vanished into the building as me and the inspector waited on the street with the body. He went to each apartment on each floor and opened up the windows. Once the windows were open, he would look down at us and close the window back up. He did this to every window in every apartment except the top floor. When he was done, he joined us on the street.

"What are you thinking, Mr. Holmes?" The inspector asked him.

"I think this was a murder, inspector, not a suicide." Sherlock stated. "I believe this man was pushed out of one of the windows."

How does Sherlock know the man was murdered?

The Case of the Frosted Glass

Sherlock and I had just sat down to a spot of tea at 221B Baker Street when the landlord allowed the inspector to come upstairs and greet us.

"Mr. Holmes, Dr. Watson," he said as he removed his hat and bowed his head to each of us.

"Inspector, to what do we owe the pleasure of your company?" Holmes asked.

"I have a strange case for you, Mr. Holmes," the inspector explained as he sat down with us for tea. "In fact, the boys and I have already solved it and arrested the criminal. I was wondering if you would be able to solve it yourself. It was quite the tricky case for us so it should be a piece of cake for you."

"I'm sure Sherlock will enjoy the challenge," I assured the inspector.

"Very well, I'll give it my best. What is the case, Inspector?"

"A man called us the other day to say that he found his friend dead in his cabin out in the woods. His story is that he was going to visit him one night. He got to the cabin and saw that a light was on inside and assumed that his friend was home. He knocked on the door and rang the bell, yet there was no answer. He went to the window of the lit room to look inside. The windows were frosted because it was winter, but he blew air on it and wiped the frost away. He saw his friend's dead body lying on the floor inside and that was when he called us." The inspector paused for a while to allow the information to sink in. "Now we already know who the killer is. I was wondering if you could figure it out."

"It's a simple case, Inspector." Sherlock stated. "It was of course the man that called the police who murdered his friend."

"How could you know that?" I asked.

How did he know?

The Case of the Wrong Door

Sherlock and I were on our second trip to Paris together. Sherlock loved his past trip there so much that he insisted we take another trip together. We arrived at our hotel room and I helped Sherlock carry his bags to his room before heading to mine.

I placed his bags down while Sherlock closed the door.

"I don't suppose you'll help me unpack?" Sherlock asked me.

"Why would you unpack, we're only staying here for a week."

"Do you expect me to live out of a suitcase, Watson? How uncivilized, indeed."

I was about to reply when there was a knock at the door. I was sure that I brought all the luggage up, so it couldn't have been a hotel employee. Sherlock went to open the door.

"Hello?" Sherlock said to the man on the other side.

"Oh! Sorry about that." The rather strange man on the other side of the door said. "I thought this was my room, but I must have gotten the wrong floor or something. My mistake. Have a nice day!"

The man walked away and Sherlock closed and locked the door.

"Watson, call the front desk and have them send security up. Tell them there's a thief in the hotel."

How did he know the man was a thief?

The Case of the Thorny Bush

There was another robbery at the Bank of England and, this time, a bag of gold bars was stolen. The robber ran into the park nearby and threw the bag of gold into a bush. He was being pursued by the police, but when the police found the gold hidden in the bush, the thief was already gone. The police have several suspects, but no evidence. That's why they called Sherlock and I down to the park to inspect the case ourselves.

"Mr. Holmes, Dr. Watson, thank you both for coming." The inspector greeted us. "I'm glad you agreed to lend your skills to the case. I know you had a successful case similar to this in the past. Back then, it was the thief that was hiding. This time, what was stolen has been hidden and the thief has completely disappeared."

"Yes, this seems like a strange case, indeed." Sherlock stated. "You said you had a list of suspects?"

"Yes! We rounded them up and they're over there waiting for you."

"Brilliant! First, would you mind showing me where the bag of gold was found?"

The inspector led us to the bush where they found the bag of gold the thief had dumped. Sherlock leaned in close to the bush and attempted to reach his hand inside.

"Careful, Mr. Holmes!" The inspector warned. "That bush is riddled with thorns. My officer cut himself badly pulling the bag out of there."

"Thank you, Inspector. I'll keep that in mind." Sherlock examined the bush for a moment, then turned around. "Now, let's have a look at our suspects."

The inspector led us to the suspects who were standing in the middle of the park. They were guarded by police officers. Sherlock examined each of the suspects. He looked at their clothes and their hands for any evidence. I stood back and watched him work. This was the way I learned.

"Do you want to ask any of them some questions?" The inspector asked Sherlock.

"No, that won't be necessary, Inspector." He pointed to one of the suspects. "This is your bank robber, you can arrest him."

SHERLOCK PUZZLE BOOK (VOLUME 4)

How did Sherlock know who the bank robber was?

The Case of the Stingy Farmer

"Watson, shall I test your skills of deduction?" Sherlock asked me one morning while we were out and about. "I think you've come a long way since I first met you and your skills have improved a lot. However, you should always practice as much as possible. Your mind is a muscle and a muscle needs constant exercise to grow."

"Okay then, Sherlock," I said. "I'm sure I'll enjoy the exercise. What kind of test are you thinking of?"

"A question, or a word puzzle for you to solve. It was actually something I read in the paper the other day."

"Alright, I'm ready."

"Living somewhere out in the countryside is a very stingy farmer. He has money but he would prefer not to spend it. He once asked his son to go buy him four things. He asked him to buy something for them to eat, something for them to drink, something that they can plant, and something they can feed the pigs in the barn." Sherlock paused and looked at me to see if I was getting all of the information. I nodded and he continued, "Now, the farmer asked his son to buy all of this but he only gave him enough money to buy one thing. What can the farmer's son buy that will give his father the four things he asked for while only buying one thing?"

"That's a tricky one, Sherlock. Although I'm sure you've already solved it."

I thought hard about what the answer might be. Knowing Sherlock, I knew it was something simple and obvious.

What can the farmer's son buy?

The Case of the Failed Suicide

and the Accidental Murder

"This is a crazy case, Mr. Holmes, and it's got me and the other inspectors completely stumped." The inspector told us as he led us into his office at Scotland Yard. "I'll try to explain the details of the situation to you as best as I can, but I'm still confused by it all."

"Take your time, Inspector, and talk slowly." Sherlock told him.

We all sat down and the inspector began his story.

"Earlier yesterday morning, a man was standing at the top of a building, preparing to jump. We were alerted straight away, so, with the help of the fire department, we had a net set up to catch the young man. Now, the man jumped from the roof of the building but when he landed in the net, he was dead."

"Dead?" I interrupted. "How?"

"He was shot in the head! Now, we did some investigation, and while the young man was on the roof, a husband was threatening his wife with a pistol on the eighth floor. As the young man jumped from the roof and past the window of the eighth floor, the husband pulled the trigger and fired his pistol at his wife. He missed his wife and the bullet went straight out the window and hit the young man in the head, killing him instantly."

"Wow, what a coincidence." I gasped.

"It gets stranger. We arrested the husband on charges of murder, but he stated that he didn't even know the gun was loaded. He said that he always kept his pistol unloaded and that he was merely trying to threaten his wife."

"Who loaded the pistol?" Sherlock asked him.

"After some investigation, we found that it was the son of the husband and wife that loaded the pistol. He was angry at his mother for cutting off his financial support. He hoped that his father would get angry one day and use the gun to threaten his mother with what his father thought was an unloaded gun. He hoped that his father would accidentally murder his mother and he would get away with it."

"This is a strange case, indeed," I told the inspector, "but what is it you want from us?"

SHERLOCK PUZZLE BOOK (VOLUME 4)

"Who should I arrest and why?" The inspector stood up and began to pace behind his desk. "I'm not sure if I should rule this a suicide, murder, or accident, and I have no idea who I should arrest, and for what?"

What should the death be ruled as, and who should be arrested and why?

The Case of the Fake War Story

The tale of how Sherlock debunked an old man's war story is quite the tale, indeed. I was there myself in order to witness the event. This sweet old man loved telling the story of how he earned a reward for bravery after saving some of his men from an explosion. He was telling this same story to his grandchildren in the park while Sherlock and I were walking past.

"I remember the day as clearly as I remember yesterday," the old man spoke to his grandchildren. "We were behind enemy lines, stalking some enemies we saw on the other side of the bushes. We were in northern France when it happened."

Sherlock overheard the man and stopped behind him to listen to the tale. I stopped beside him and listened as well.

"I spotted an enemy soldier in the distance and he spotted me, too. He threw a grenade at me and my men and it landed right by my feet. I picked it up and threw it away just before it exploded. For this act of bravery, I was rewarded with a sword engraved with the words 'For Your Display of Heroism and Bravery in World War 1.' I was very proud of this achievement and I hung the sword up on my mantelpiece to show it to the world."

"That's a nice story," Sherlock chimed in. "Too bad it's a lie and your sword is a fake."

The old man stood up, enraged, and yelled at Sherlock.

"How dare you? How dare you call me a liar and my reward a fake? I fought in the war for people like you and now you stand there and tell me I am lying!"

"It is a lie and you know it. You shouldn't spread fake stories of the war. You should instead be proud of the real deeds you performed during the war."

"Sherlock," I interrupted before the old man got too angry. "How can you know for certain he isn't telling the truth?"

How did Sherlock know the sword was fake and the story a lie?

The Case of the Fork in the Road

I was in the driver's seat while Sherlock read a map beside me. We were on our way to a crime scene somewhere out in the country, and the inspector had given us directions. Somewhere along the line I took a wrong turn, and we were lost for the rest of the night. We came to a forked road and neither of us could make head or tail of the map, so we didn't know which road to go down - the left or the right.

Instead of driving further and getting more lost, I called the inspector and told him we were lost.

"This reminds me of a story I read," Sherlock said as we waited in the car for the inspector to find us. "It involved a fork road and two brothers, one whom would always tell the truth and one whom would always lie."

"What was the story about?"

"You come to a fork road and you don't know which road to take. One road leads to certain death and the other leads to safety. The two brothers know which road is which, but as I said before one of them lies and one of them tells the truth. You don't know which brother is which. You can ask both brothers a single question in order to find the right road."

"That is an interesting story, Sherlock." I told him. "What question do they ask in the story?"

"What question would you ask, Watson? I wonder how quick you can solve the mystery. What question would you ask both the brothers in order to find the road that leads you to safety?"

"That is a difficult one," I said as I began to think of an answer.

What question should you ask the brothers?

The Case of the Disappearing Murder Weapon

We followed behind the inspector's car once he rescued us after we got lost. We made our way to the crime scene, which was an expensive resort out in the countryside. The resort recently found one of their residents dead in the sauna with three of his friends.

The inspector told us that he needed our help for this case because of a problem with the murder weapon. We walked into the sauna to find the murdered man face down on the floor in a puddle of blood.

"What is the problem, Inspector?" Sherlock asked as I examined the body.

"This man was stabbed in the stomach with something very sharp and thin," I concluded after my examination. "You said you were having a problem with the murder weapon, inspector."

"Yes, it's disappeared!" The inspector threw his hands up in the air. "The murder victim walked in here with three of his friends about an hour ago. They were all sitting on the bench one second and then steam filled the room. When the steam cleared, he was dead on the floor and there was no murder weapon or any witnesses. We only have three suspects."

"The three friends who walked in here with the murder victim, I presume." Sherlock said and the inspector nodded.

"All of the suspects state that they didn't see anyone bring in a weapon of any kind and none of them saw what happened."

"What did the suspects bring in here with them?" I asked.

"One brought a book, one brought a flask, and one brought a mask for his eyes. None of those could have been used to kill the victim."

"Then the weapon was hidden in some way and disposed of afterwards." Sherlock stated. "The question is what was used to kill this man. If we answer that, we will have the answers to the rest of our questions."

What was the murder weapon?

The Case of the Impossible Escape

"Sherlock," I called for him as I walked into the living room of our home at 221B Baker Street. "I found a rather difficult puzzle in the newspaper that I think you may enjoy. Perhaps it will get your mind off the fact that the inspector hasn't called for your help in a few weeks."

Sherlock came out of his room and collapsed onto the couch.

"I'm bored, Watson. No new cases and no new clients in weeks! My mind needs constant exercise or I'm afraid I will grow slow and dumb like most other people."

"Well, see if you can solve this puzzle," I handed him the newspaper. "I've already solved it so it should be child's play for you."

Sherlock picked the newspaper up and read the puzzle out loud.

"See if you can help the young boy escape his fate. He is dangling from a branch high in a tree. The tree has been cut half way through by an axe, so if he stays there for too long, it will fall. The axe is still at the base of the tree, sitting next to a lion waiting to eat the boy if he climbs down. There is a snake hanging on the branch near the boy, waiting to bite him if he doesn't act fast enough. Below him is a river with two crocodiles waiting to eat him if he falls into the water. How can the young boy escape his fate?"

"It's a tough one," I teased Sherlock.

I knew he could solve it and I watched him put the newspaper down and lean back in his chair. He thought long and hard to find the answer.

How can the boy escape his fate?

The Case of the Man who Cheated Death

I was reading a book, as I usually do on a Sunday afternoon, after Sherlock and I had returned from our afternoon walk. The book was very interesting and it contained many riddles. Sherlock never showed any interest in it, because all of the riddles were too easy for him, but I came across a particularly difficult one that Sunday afternoon.

I read the riddle myself and laughed at how difficult it seemed. When I found the answer, I laughed at how simple it was. I had to share this riddle with Sherlock and see if he could solve it as I was able to.

"Sherlock, won't you come here for a moment?" I called to him.

Sherlock came out of his room and joined me in the living room.

"Watson, you know I enjoy a bit of quiet time after our Sunday walk," he said as he walked up to me. "What is so important that you would interrupt my quiet time?"

"It's just a difficult riddle that I think you'll find entertaining and a good exercise for your mind, but if you're not interested, I can keep it to myself."

"Alright, I'll humor you," Sherlock muttered.

"The riddle is known as 'The Man who Cheated Death'. Here's how it goes: There once was a man who had three sons. He was very old and, one day, Death came to collect his soul. The oldest son begged Death to give his father another three years to live and Death granted his wish. The years passed and Death came to collect the man's soul once again. This time, the middle son asked Death to give his father one more year to live. Death was kind and so he granted the middle son's wish. When the year was up, Death returned again to collect the man's soul. The youngest son asked Death for one more favor. He lit a candle and asked Death to give his father until the wick of the candle was completely burnt away to live. Death looked at the candle and then accepted the youngest son's wish. Death left and he never returned. Why did Death never return?"

I looked to Sherlock and I could see that he was thinking.

Why did Death never return?

The Case of the Crazed Kidnapper's Code

It is strange to tell the story of when Sherlock was once kidnapped by one of his crazed fans. He had been attacked by many fans, but this was the first time he was taken hostage.

Sherlock told me the tale with a lot of detail, mostly because he thought himself very clever for saving himself instead of waiting for the police and I to rescue him.

Sherlock said that the kidnapper placed him in a cell and told him he needed to solve a puzzle to unlock his cell. The lock on his cell needed seven sets of numbers to unlock it. His kidnapper gave him a piece of paper with the beginning of the code for the lock and told him to find the last set of numbers.

The paper read: 1, 11, 21, 1211, 111221, 312211. Find the last set of numbers to unlock the door.

Sherlock brags about how easy it was for him to solve the puzzle and release himself from his cell. He'll never let me forget it and he even asked me to solve the puzzle myself when he returned. He said that the numbers form a pattern and to solve the puzzle you needed to find the next number in the pattern.

What is the next number in the pattern?

The Case of the Lost Survivalist

A survival enthusiast was lost in the woods and he had managed to get a signal high on the mountain top. He used his signal and a failing battery life to call Sherlock Holmes, who was the man he trusted the most.

Sherlock and this man are old friends and he always calls Sherlock when he is in need of help. He told Sherlock where he was the last time he looked at his map, but he stumbled off the trial, fell into a river, and lost his map. His clothes and all of his supplies were soaked in the cold water. Now he is not sure where he is, but he hasn't moved far from his last known location.

I called the police while Sherlock stayed on the phone with him.

"Where are you now?" Sherlock asked him.

"I'm at the top of a mountain, I think. I think I can see a cabin in the distance. I'm going to go see if there is someone inside of it." There was a moment of silence on the other end of the phone. "The cabin is empty, but, at least, I can try staying warm in here. I have some matches in my pocket, so I'll try to light a fire in the fireplace."

"That sounds like a good idea. After that, you should stay put until the police can send someone out there to find you." Sherlock instructed.

"My battery is about to die, Sherlock. Thank you for your help. I'll see you soon."

The phone went dead and all Sherlock and I could do was wait. We waited all night long, but in the morning, the inspector gave us a call. They found Sherlock's friend in a cabin in the mountains, but he was dead.

How did he die?

The Case of the Copycat Killer

There was a killer on the loose and the police were close to capturing him. Sherlock and I had been a part of the case from the beginning, and it was partly because of us that they were close to capturing the killer now.

All of the evidence led us to a warehouse near the edge of the city. The police surrounded the premises and we waited on the outskirts with the inspector. We knew that the killer had many spies around the city, so we suspected that he knew we were coming for him.

We watched as the police stormed the warehouse and arrested everyone within it. It wasn't long before they called us inside with a problem. As we entered the warehouse, the problem became quite obvious. They had caught the killer, along with seven other copy cats that looked and were dressed just like him.

They all looked so similar that the police weren't sure which one was the real killer. They looked to Sherlock to solve the mystery, and Sherlock looked to me.

"Why don't you solve this one, Watson?" He told me. "Give your mind a bit of an exercise."

I wasn't sure of myself at first, but I studied the eight copycat killers carefully and eventually, I found the real killer. I pointed him out to the police and they arrested him immediately.

How did I spot the real killer?

The Case of the Sudden Second Funeral

Sherlock insisted I accompany him to his friend's funeral and I, of course, accepted. It seemed like only yesterday that he got lost in the woods and died, but it took his family nearly five weeks to set up the funeral.

On that day, I met a lot of Sherlock's friends and the family of the deceased. His sister was infatuated with Sherlock, which I already knew because Sherlock warned me before we arrived.

She followed us around all day and took every opportunity to talk to him instead of mourning her brother's death. It was strange, but Sherlock has accumulated many strange fans over the years and I have learned to deal with them.

When the funeral was over, we went home and had tea. I asked Sherlock why he indulged the mad woman instead of ignoring her and he said that she was the sister of his friend, so he felt obliged to.

A few days later, we received a call from the sister of his dead friend. She informed us that her father had been missing for a few days and is presumed dead. She said they were arranging a funeral and asked if Sherlock would attend it. Sherlock told me the news and I found it quite strange. Thankfully, so did Sherlock.

"I believe the father of my friend was killed, Watson." Sherlock stated.

"How can you be certain?" I asked.

"It's strange how he would die only a day after the funeral of his son." Sherlock explained. "I believe that he was killed by his daughter."

"Do you mean the girl from the funeral?" I was of course confused. "Why would she murder her own father a day after her brother's funeral?"

Why did the girl murder her father?

The Case of the Day in Court

Sherlock had agreed to testify against the young girl who murdered her father. Sherlock was close with the father and his son. He made it his duty to see that the young girl would pay for her crime. However, she had a very good lawyer, and he was doing everything in his power to convince the jury that the young girl was innocent.

"This young girl's father is not dead, he is simply missing." The lawyer stated. "His body has not been found and this whole case is hanging by a thread. For all we know, her father could walk right through that door in the next minute!" The lawyer stunned everyone with his closing statement as he pointed to the door at the back of the courtroom.

The jury, the judge, and everyone in the court looked towards the door. Sherlock kept his eyes on the young girl and the young girl looked at the judge. The minute passed and nobody walked through the door. Afterwards, Sherlock stood up to give his statement.

When Sherlock finished his statement, the jury gave the young woman a guilty verdict.

Why did the jury convict the young woman?

The Case of the Untouched Vehicle

The inspector came to visit us at 221B Baker Street as he usually did if he hadn't seen us in a while. We sat down for tea and he offered to tell us about his most recent case. Sherlock was eager as he knew it meant that there was a mystery to be solved.

"The police found a man shot dead in his convertible in the middle of the night," the inspector explained. "We examined the car and there was no gunpowder in the car or on the dead man's body. This means that the gun had to be fired from outside the car. Now, all the windows were rolled up and the doors were locked, yet someone managed to shoot the man inside the car while standing outside the car. We checked the whole car and the only bullet holes we found were in the dead man's body."

"Interesting," Sherlock whispered.

"How did the killer manage to shoot the man inside the car?" The inspector asked. "I'm sure you can figure this one out, Mr. Holmes."

I drank my tea as Sherlock thought of the best answer to the puzzling crime.

How was the man shot?

The Case of the Murdered Chemist

Through the years, I came to learn of Sherlock's many talents and his many friends. One of his friends was a famous chemist who was particularly good at his job. Sherlock once told me he learned everything he knew about chemistry from this one friend.

One day, we received a call from the inspector and he informed us that the chemist had been murdered and he left a note for Sherlock at the crime scene. Sherlock knew that the note would lead to his friend's murderer. We made our way down there straight away.

As soon as we arrived at the scene, the inspector handed Sherlock the note. He read it a couple times over. It read:

"Sherlock, my friend, I know only you can catch my murderers. Remember everything I taught you when reading this note. Their names are 26, 3, 58 and 28, 27, 57, 16. Catch them and make them pay, my dear friend."

At first the note was a mystery, but it didn't stay that way for long. In a few minutes, Sherlock was able to give the inspector the names of his friend's murderers.

Who murdered the chemist?

The Case of the Captain's Missing Ring

A Japanese cargo ship was docked in the city harbor and preparing to leave on a long journey. I had never seen a Japanese ship, so Sherlock and I took a trip down to the harbor to see it for ourselves. We watched it from a distance for a bit before Sherlock used his famous title to get us a closer look.

We were standing right beside the ship when we heard the captain of the ship shouting at a few members of his crew. They were all lined up outside the front of the ship.

The captain shouted, "Which one of you is a thief? Which one of you stole my ring?"

Sherlock and I made our way to the captain and we intervened.

"Sorry to interrupt," Sherlock said as we walked to the front of the ship. "I'm detective Sherlock Holmes and this is my good friend Dr. John Watson. I couldn't help but overhear you. Someone stole your ring?"

"The captain turned to face us, "Yes, that's what I believed happened, Detective. I had taken my ring off before I got into the shower only a few minutes ago. When I got out of the shower, my ring was gone. A member of my crew has stolen it, I'm sure, but I don't know which one did it."

"May I ask your crew some questions?"

"Go ahead, Detective, maybe you can find the thief among my crew."

Sherlock asked them all what they were doing at the time the ring went missing.

The chef said he was in the fridge room making sure they had enough stock for their long trip ahead.

The radio officer said he was sending a message to their company, informing them of their departure.

The engineer said he was preparing the engine for their trip.

The navigation officer said he was double checking their route on the maps.

The seaman said he was correcting the flag up on the mast because it had been hung upside down by accident.

"The seaman stole your ring," Sherlock stated straight away.

How did he know?

ANSWERS

(Answers) The Case of the Murdered Architect

At first, the case posed quite a difficult question for me. I thought hard about it, but after listening to Sherlock's advice, it became very clear.

"I see now, the prime suspect must be the maid," I concluded and saw Sherlock smirk with pride. "She stated that she was cleaning the house, which is a sound alibi. However, she mentioned one of her duties is to sweep the corners."

"This is, of course, an impossible feat to pull off, given that the house is perfectly round and no corners exist inside of it." Sherlock continued from me. "Officer, I think you'll find that the maid is the one who murdered Mr. Arch Digger. I suggest you arrest her and run her fingerprints against those on the murder weapon."

"Well done, Mr. Holmes," I congratulated the detective.

"Well done to you, Watson, you solved the case, not I."

SHERLOCK PUZZLE BOOK (VOLUME 4)

It was a strange case, but in the end, the evidence revealed that the maid murdered the architect.

(Answers) The Case of the Vanishing Bank Robber

I looked at the frozen-over lake and the man-sized hole in the surface of it. The pile of wet clothes lay right beside the hole. I breathed in, and the air around me was cold enough to turn my breath into mist.

"I see now what has happened," I began, "the bank robber ran this way after escaping the capture of the police and he fell through the frozen lake. The surface is frozen over, but beneath it, the water is not. The robber then pulled himself from the lake, removed his clothes, and hid somewhere nearby."

"Exactly!" Sherlock clapped his hands. "How is it you know the bank robber is still nearby?"

"His clothes are still soaked. The air is extremely cold; if the clothes were lying there for long enough they would be frozen like the surface of the lake. They are still wet, which means they haven't even been there for a few minutes. Given that amount of time, the bank robber couldn't have gone far, so he must still be hiding in the park somewhere."

"Well done, Watson!" Sherlock turned to the officers. "There you have it, your bank robber is still in the park, probably hiding somewhere in the bushes."

Sherlock managed to outsmart everyone again. In the end, it was quite clear to me and the officers that, given all of the available evidence, the bank robber had to be hiding somewhere nearby.

(Answers) The Case of the Slow Drinker

"Both men were drinking from the same bottle of whiskey, but only one of the men died, so it is safe to assume that the whiskey itself was not poisoned." Sherlock explained. "However, we know that he could have been poisoned by the ice in the glass."

"Both men had ice in their glass, Sherlock." I pointed out. "Would that not mean that the other man would be poisoned, too?"

"Not necessarily. You see, the dead man only managed to drink one glass of whiskey in the time it took his friend to drink six. He is a slow drinker, and his friend is a fast one. His friend drank his whiskey so fast that he didn't give the ice enough time to melt. Therefore, he didn't actually drink any of the poison inside the ice. However, the dead man drank his whiskey slowly, giving his ice an appropriate time to melt, and so he ingested the poison within it."

"So he was poisoned!" The officer said, stunned by Sherlock's explanation.

"In fact, both men were meant to be poisoned," Sherlock added. "Only one man was killed because he was a slow drinker. I suggest arresting the barman, as he was probably the one that poisoned the ice in their glasses."

The case was closed before it was even opened, thanks to Sherlock and his ability to think outside the box.

(Answers) The Case of the Dead Man in the Snow

"You should be looking for someone in a wheelchair, they are your murderer," I informed the police.

It was an obvious conclusion to come to, once I examined the crime scene as a whole. There were the dead man's footprints leading up to his body and there were no other markings in the snow besides the parallel lines. I concluded that those markings belonged to the wheels on a wheelchair. Since they are the only other markings in the snow, that meant that the murderer was someone in a wheelchair.

(Answers) The Case of the Missing Mail

"Sherlock, how could you possibly know that?" I asked.

Both I and the inspector were shocked that he had so easily come to this conclusion.

"What day is it today, Watson?" Sherlock asked.

"It's Thursday, of course."

"Exactly, and yet when I look at the murder victim's collection of mail, I see only a few letters and the newspaper from Monday."

"What does that have to do with anything?" The inspector asked.

"The mail from Tuesday and Wednesday are missing. The mailman didn't deliver any mail to this house on those two days because he was already aware that the occupant was dead inside, making him the obvious murderer." Sherlock smiled proudly. "The only reason he decided to report the dead body to the police this morning was because the smell was becoming too strong to ignore. He was probably afraid that someone else would report the smell. If he does it, then he looks less guilty than he clearly is."

"That makes sense," the inspector agreed. "Arrest the mailman!"

"Very well done, Mr. Holmes." I congratulated him. "I would never have guessed it was the mailman."

(Answers) The Case of the Two Wives

"It's obvious from that photo that she is your wife because she is the only woman of the two wearing a ring - a wedding ring, to be precise." Sherlock explained. "If you look at the photo closely, you can see that her wedding ring is similar to your own, Mr. Harley."

Benny Harley and I examined the photo once again. Sherlock was correct as usual. The woman in the plain skirt and shirt was wearing a wedding ring, and the woman in the red dress was not.

"The woman in the red dress tried to make herself look as though she is the wife of a rich businessman, but she failed by not even attempting to wear a wedding ring to prove it."

"Thank you, Mr. Holmes," Benny Harley said, relieved. "Thank you very much."

"I must say, Sherlock, I am impressed." I congratulated him. "I would never have thought to look for a wedding ring. How obvious!"

(Answers) The Case of the Coded Kidnapper

"I think I've deciphered it, Holmes." I stated, quite proud of myself. "I believe the kidnapper to be John Blacksmith."

"How can you be certain?" The inspector asked.

"Yes, Watson, please share with us your methods of deduction."

I took the note and showed it to Sherlock and the inspector.

"If we take the first letter of January we get the letter J. If we take the fourth letter of October then we get the letter O. If we take the fifth letter of March we get the letter H. Finally if we take the third letter of June then we get the letter N. Put those together and they spell out John. Therefore, Harold Green was trying to tell us that his kidnapper is John Blacksmith."

"Very well, we'll arrest him straight away and ask him where he's taken Harold Green."

"Good work, Watson. Your deduction skills are coming along nicely."

"Thank you, Sherlock."

(Answers) The Case of the Unfortunate Camping Trip

"Alex is the killer," I stated.

"How can you know for sure?" The inspector asked me.

"The evidence speaks for itself. You see, Steven Brook swears that he was stuck at work for the past seven days and hasn't seen his brother since he left for the camping trip. However, Alex went with Tim Brook on the camping trip but he claims he got lost the first night and has been stuck in the woods for the past seven days."

"Yes," the inspector sighed, "I know all that. How do you know Alex murdered Tim Brook?"

"Alex is lying about being lost in the woods for the past seven days, and so he must be lying to conceal the fact that he is the murderer." I stated proudly.

"Well done, Watson!" Sherlock clapped his hands softly. "How did you come to the conclusion that Alex was lying?"

"It was his appearance, you see, that gave it away." I gestured to the clothes that Alex was wearing. "His hair looks messy and uncombed, which could indicate that he hasn't been able to care for it for a while. However, his pants and shirt are clean and undamaged. If a man had been lost wandering around the woods for seven days, you would expect to see dirt on his clothes or even rips and tears. Alex's clothes are fresh and spotless, as if he pulled them out from his closet this morning."

"Outstanding!" the inspector's mouth was hanging open. "We would never have guessed it. We'll start questioning Alex straight away. Thank you for your assistance, Mr. Holmes and Dr. Watson."

"Any time, Inspector!" I replied.

(Answers) The Case of the Strange Note

"The note clearly reads '? Hollow,' twice in a row. If you read that out loud what would you hear?"

"Question Mark Hollow," my eyes lit up as I realized what Sherlock was getting at. "I understand now. The question mark in the note should be put into full words to get the answer. It is telling you to question someone named Mark Hollow."

"Yes! He is the one that threw the stone through my window!" Sherlock stomped back inside the house. "Get the phone book, we need to find someone named Mark Hollow and send him the bill for the window."

(Answers) The Case of the Missing Hiker

"I called the travel agency to ask what kind of booking Aleister Barley made for himself and his business partner," Sherlock explained. "That is how I managed to decipher that Aleister Barley planned that trip so he could murder his business partner. The travel agency said that he booked a round trip ticket and a one-way ticket."

"I don't think I follow you, Sherlock."

"A one-way trip would cost a lot less than a round trip. Aleister Barley bought a round trip ticket for himself but only purchased a one-way ticket for his business partner. He didn't see the use in spending the extra money on two round trip tickets when he knew that his business partner would not be making the trip back. He planned on killing him and leaving him in Japan, so he didn't feel it necessary to buy him a round trip ticket."

"My goodness!" I got up instantly and fetched my coat. "We must inform the inspector at Scotland Yard at once!"

"I'm way ahead of you, Watson."

(Answers) The Case of the Sand Smuggler

"You have?" The inspector sounded shocked and impressed. "How is he doing it?"

"You've searched the man and the two bags that he carries each time he crosses the border; next time I suggest you search his motorcycle." I explained. "The man carries the bags of sand to distract you. He wants you to believe that he is hiding something in his bags so that you don't think to look any further. Whatever he is smuggling is hidden somewhere on or inside his motorcycle."

"Outstanding!" The inspector's mouth dropped open.

"Very well done, Watson." Sherlock gave me a pat on the back. "Of course, I already deduced that myself, but I was hoping you would be brave enough to accept the challenge. It really was an easy one this time."

"It was easy but only once I put a bit of thought into it," I agreed.

(Answers) The Case of the Murder in Disguise

"It's actually quite simple," Sherlock explained to the angry inspector. "You stated that neither you nor of your men touched the cassette recorder. Is that correct?"

"Yes!"

"We can also assume that nobody else touched it except for the dead man, if he committed suicide."

"Which he did!"

"No he didn't, dear Inspector. You see, how can a dead man rewind the tape?"

Both the inspector and I stared down at the tape and then looked back to Sherlock.

"On the tape, we can hear the gunshot. This is supposed to be the victim shooting himself after finishing his suicide note. However, if that was the case, then there would have been no one to stop the tape and rewind it back to the beginning so that I could simply play it now. The tape would have carried on recording the silence of the room and be stuck at the end."

Sherlock paused for a moment to take in the shocked expression on the inspector's face.

"Therefore, we can conclude that this is not a suicide, but rather a murder disguised as one. The murderer shot the victim at the end of his suicide note and he stopped the tape. He then staged it as a suicide and rewound the tape back to the beginning. It's elementary!"

"Well, there goes my chance at an easy night of paperwork," the inspector sighed.

(Answers) The Case of the Guilty Husband

"It was quite simple actually. You basically confessed to the crime," Sherlock explained. "You said that during the phone call, your housekeeper stated that something terrible has happened to your wife and that she was sent to intensive care. If these are the exact words that she used, she never mentioned a gunshot. Yet you came running in here, claiming that someone has shot your wife. How would you know that if you are not the one that shot her?"

"Damn you, Sherlock Holmes!" The man spat at him.

"That is a very dramatic story," I told Sherlock. "I'm sure the man didn't actually spit at you, though."

(Answers) The Case of the Murdering Sons

"Sherlock," I called him over to the body. "I believe by examining the evidence on the victim's body that we can conclude which of the brothers are lying."

"Yes of course, Watson." Sherlock looked down at the body. "What have you come up with?"

"This man was shot in the forehead and killed, which means the killer needed to be standing in front of him to have done it."

"I see," Sherlock smiled and walked back to the inspector and the brothers. He pointed at the older brothers Jack and John. "Arrest these two for the murder of their father."

"What is the meaning of this?" Jack hissed as the inspector put the cuffs on him and John.

"Watson, would you like to explain your findings?"

"You stated that it was your little brother James that shot and killed your father," I explained to them.

"You said your father was walking up the stairs when James walked in through the front door and shot him. If that had actually happened then he would have shot your father in the back. However, your father was shot in the forehead. Whoever shot him had to be standing in front of him at the time."

"Obviously you two are lying and trying to frame your little brother for the murder," Sherlock added.

The inspector arrested Jack and John; James was free to go, being the only innocent one of the three.

(Answers) The Case of the Serial Killer

"What if the pills are not actually poisonous," I suggested.

Sherlock's eyes widened and his mouth dropped open. "Yes of course!" He jumped out of his seat. "The pills contain no poison but the glass of water does. The serial killer gives his victims and himself a harmless pill but the victim's glass of water is laced with poison, while the killer's is not. How did you know, Watson?"

I shrugged my shoulders and smiled, "It was just a guess."

"I've been trying to solve this for three weeks! I can't believe you solved it in a minute. Perhaps I should also go on a vacation."

(Answers) The Case of the Stolen Bracelet

"Mr. Holmes, I demand to know why you think poor Catherine is guilty when she is the victim of a crime." The investigator was beginning to doubt Sherlock's famed skills.

"If you look at the crime scene, you will find the answers," Sherlock explained. "The bedroom window was broken, and yet there is no glass on the floor. This means that the window was broken from the inside, not the outside, so it couldn't have been the thief's point of entrance. Furthermore, the rest of the room is clean and untouched while the muddy footprints head straight to the dresser where Catherine keeps her bracelet. The thief knew what he was looking for, so he didn't see a need in searching the rest of the room."

Sherlock paused and smiled at his brilliance, "It's safe to say that Catherine stole the bracelet herself. She broke the window from the inside out and left the muddy footprints to make it seem like a robbery."

"Wow, I am impressed Mr. Holmes. I guess the stories are true. You are a brilliant detective."

(Answers) The Case of the Prison Escape

"I'll admit, that was a hard challenge, Watson, but I've figured it out." Sherlock stated.

"Have you?"

"Yes, it's quite simple and I would escape in the same way if put under the same circumstances." Sherlock explained. "The man used the shovel to pile the dirt from the floor up so he could climb it and reach the window. He then climbed through the window and escaped."

"Wow! Your trip to Paris really has sharpened your skills. I'm impressed."

"Of course you are, Watson!" Sherlock smiled, proud of himself and his skills.

(Answers) The Case of the Empty Room

"How can you be sure it's a suicide, Mr. Holmes?" The inspector asked. "There is no way for her to have been able to hang herself from the ceiling, so someone else must have done it."

"I know it is a suicide because all of the evidence points towards it. The doors and windows were locked from the inside and the victim's neck was bruised and broken from the rope."

"Then how did she get up there in order to hang herself?"

"She stood on a block of ice," Sherlock stated with a straight face. "If you notice the dark, damp spot underneath the body, you will see that it is where the ice block melted and the water soaked into the wooden floorboards."

The inspector and I examined the floor and found that Sherlock was correct.

"The woman committed suicide but she probably wanted to make it look like a murder. She stepped up on a block of ice and hung herself. Over time, the ice melted away and the water soaked into the floorboards, making it look as though the room was empty. This would lead anyone to conclude that she couldn't have killed herself and must have been murdered. However, if you look closely enough, the evidence will always tell you the truth."

(Answers) The Case of the Fly in his Tea

"It's simple, you see this cup is still warm." Sherlock explained. "It's warm from when my friend, Watson poured the tea in it. The tea was so hot that it burned his hand and so it warmed up the cup. The cup also still carries the slight aroma of tea."

The waitress took the cup and left the table with her cheeks red from embarrassment.

"Well done, Sherlock. I am impressed, but it really wasn't that much of a bother." I said.

"Nonsense, Watson. It's entirely unhygienic. I certainly won't be coming to this café again, even if we have to wait for a train nearby."

(Answers) The Case of the Full House

"Well, don't leave us in anticipation. Who is it?" The inspector asked Sherlock.

He pointed his finger at Jenny, "Her alibi is false, therefore I suggest that she is the murderer."

"How can you be for sure that she is lying?" I asked him.

"Look at her hands," he walked up to Jenny and held up one of her hands for the room to see. "They are smooth, clean, and undamaged, yet she claims that she has been in a swimming pool for three hours. If that were true, the skin on her fingers would be heavily wrinkled."

"You're right!" The inspector bowed his head in shame. "How did I miss that?"

"Simple. You weren't looking for it."

(Answers) The Case of the Suspicious Death

"Mr. Holmes, how can you be certain?" the inspector asked him.

"The husband claims that he always keeps the gun safe locked and yet his wife managed to open it without forcing or breaking it," Sherlock explained. "That means that she had to have unlocked it using the key. The key can be found nowhere in the study or on the wife's body. Therefore, I conclude that if you search the husband you will find the key to the gun safe on his body."

The inspector put handcuffs on the husband and searched his body. Sherlock was right. They found the key to the gun safe in his pocket.

"It's obvious that he came home, opened the gun safe, took his own gun, and shot his wife in the head. He then staged the incident to look like a suicide." Sherlock added. "The case is closed."

"Outstanding work, Mr. Holmes!" the inspector said as he led the murderer out of the house in handcuffs.

(Answers) The Case of the Closed Windows

"Sherlock, what makes you think this man was murdered?" I asked him.

"As I walked through each apartment on each floor, I noticed something. I had to open all of the windows I looked through." Sherlock explained. "What does that mean to you, dear Watson? Surely I can trust you to solve it."

I thought for a moment, but the answer was actually quite simple.

"Oh, I see!" I said when I finally got it. "If the man had jumped from the building, then the window he jumped from would still be open. However, all of the windows were closed. He must have been pushed by someone."

"Exactly! Since dead men can't close windows, it is logical to assume that someone pushed him out of the window and then closed the window before leaving the scene of the crime. This man was murdered, Inspector!"

"Well, I'll be a monkey's uncle! I didn't think of that." The inspector rubbed his head in amazement.

"You just have to know what to look for, Inspector." Sherlock smiled, proud with himself.

(Answers) The Case of the Frosted Glass

"Honestly, Watson, it wasn't that difficult. The man gave himself away." Sherlock explained. "He said he had to blow air on the window and wipe the frost away to see inside the cabin, but that wouldn't have worked. If it was cold enough for the outside of the window to frost up, then the inside of the window would have been frosted too. The man wouldn't have been able to see through the window even after wiping the frost away, which means he wouldn't have been able to see his dead friend inside."

"Is he right, Inspector?" I asked, still stunned, myself.

The inspector looked dazed and shocked, "Yes, he is right. It took us hours to figure that out, and you did it in minutes! Eventually, one of the officers had to look through the window himself to realize that he couldn't do it."

"I'm impressed that you did it at all, Inspector. Perhaps our skills are rubbing off on you after all."

The inspector smiled and we finished our tea.

(Answers) The Case of the Wrong Door

"What?" I stood up and reached for the phone. "How can you be certain that man is a thief? He simply got the wrong door."

"It's obvious he's a thief, Watson. He knocked on the door." Sherlock explained. "If he thought that this room was his, then he would have put his key in the lock or tried to open it. He wouldn't have knocked. The only reason he knocked was to see if anyone was in here. If there was no answer, then he would have tried to break in and steal something. Are you calling the front desk?"

"Yes, Sherlock, I'm calling them now."

"Very good, I'll start unpacking in the meantime."

(Answers) The Case of the Thorny Bush

Sherlock brought the suspect forward and gestured to his clothes and his hands.

"Notice how this man's clothes are damaged along the sleeve and his hands have small cuts on them." He explained. "You said earlier, Inspector, that the bush the gold was hidden in was riddled with thorns. Your own officer cut his hand while reaching for the gold. Therefore, it is safe to assume the man who hid the gold in the bush would sustain the same injuries. Out of the many suspects you have here, this man is the only one with injuries on his hands and rips in his sleeves." Sherlock paused and looked the man up and down. "I think it's safe to assume he was the one who hid the bag of gold in the thorny bush and that is how he sustained these cuts on his hands. He robbed the Bank of England."

"Well done!" I cheered. "Very well done, Sherlock. I would never have guessed it myself."

"I think you could have, Watson. Your skills are improving every day. You just need to notice the small, insignificant information over the large, important, and sometimes obvious information."

(Answers) The Case of the Stingy Farmer

It took me a moment to figure out the answer. It was a difficult question that required me to think outside of the box and put myself in the shoes of the farmer's son.

"Should I incorporate a time limit into this little test of ours?" Sherlock asked.

"No need, Sherlock, I've already found the answer," I told him. "The farmer's son can buy a watermelon."

"A watermelon? Why would he buy that, Watson?"

"The body of the watermelon would give them something to eat, the juice of the watermelon would give them something to drink, they could plant the seeds to grow some more, and they can feed the rind to the pigs."

"Do pigs eat watermelon rind?"

"Is that part of the test?"

Sherlock roared with laughter, "No, my dear Watson, that was not part of the test. Well done, in fact. a watermelon is the correct answer."

"Thank you, Sherlock, for insisting on keeping my mind active."

(Answers) The Case of the Failed Suicide and the Accidental Murder

"Give me a moment," Sherlock muttered.

He put his hand to his mouth and leaned back in his chair. He was thinking hard. I was completely stumped by the whole thing, so I knew I would be able to help him.

"Usually, by law, if a man or woman attempts to commit suicide and their death comes as a direct cause of the actions they take to commit suicide, then that is what it is: A suicide. The man jumped from the building, with the intent of killing himself, so even though he was killed by a bullet on the way down, he still jumped. Therefore, I suggest that his death be ruled a suicide. No one needs to be arrested for that."

"Right!" The inspector collapsed in his chair. "That's a load off my mind. What about the rest of it?"

"The husband was threatening his wife with the pistol but he was under the impression that it wasn't loaded. He had no intent to actually harm his wife in any way. I don't believe you can arrest him on anything. However, their son loaded the gun with the thought that, one day, his father would accidentally shoot his mother. I suggest you arrest their son and charge him with conspiracy to commit murder."

"Wow, Mr. Holmes. You really helped me out on this one." The inspector sighed out of relief. "I was really worked up."

"I'm impressed too, Sherlock." I congratulated him.

"It just took a bit of thought, that's all, but thank you."

(Answers) The Case of the Fake War Story

The old man looked very angry and his grandchildren were scared, but Sherlock stood his ground and he wasn't about to back down. I stood between them. Sherlock was certain the old man was lying and this offended him.

"I know your story is a fake, and if you actually have a sword, it is a fake too." Sherlock told him. "I know this because, if you had been rewarded with an engraved sword, it wouldn't have the words 'World War 1' on it. At the time, they never believed that there would be another World War."

The old man's face went pale and the anger was quickly replaced by embarrassment.

"Your sword is a fake, if it were real it would simply say 'The World War,' not 'World War 1.' Am I correct?"

The old man didn't say anything. He sat back down and refused to look up at Sherlock.

SHERLOCK PUZZLE BOOK (VOLUME 4)

"Well then, Watson, should we continue our walk?"

I nodded my head, still dazed and confused by what just transpired. We continued on our walk and the old man sat in silence while his grandchildren played.

(Answers) The Case of the Fork in the Road

I thought for a while, but we had the time because the inspector hadn't found us just yet. I eventually found the answer by thinking the way Sherlock taught me to.

"You should ask both the brothers the same question," I explained. "You should ask both brothers, 'if you were your brother, which road would you say leads to safety?' and then you should take the opposite road that they tell you to take."

"Interesting answer," Sherlock muttered. "Can you explain further?"

"If you ask both brothers that question, they would give you the same answer. The brother who tells the truth would say that if he were his brother, he would tell me to take the road that leads to death, because I asked for the road that leads to safety, thus he would lie and tell me to take the road to death. The brother who lies will tell me that his brother would also tell me to take the road that leads to death. However, this brother always lies, so he is lying about what his brother would say. Therefore, I ask them this question and then take the opposite path that they told me to take."

"Well done, Watson." Sherlock clapped his hands. "I was quite confused by the story at first, but I eventually got it. I'm impressed that you figured it out yourself."

As Sherlock finished speaking, we spotted the headlights from the inspector's car behind us.

(Answers) The Case of the Disappearing Murder Weapon

"I may have an idea," I told Sherlock. "It's a crazy idea, but if someone really wants to murder someone else, they would probably do anything to make sure they get away with it."

"Go on then, Dr. Watson, tell us your thoughts," the inspector insisted.

"I think the murder weapon was an icicle, and the suspect carrying the flask used the flask to hide the icicle." I expected to hear laughter, but I didn't.

"Brilliant, Watson!" Sherlock cheered. "I would never have thought that far out the box but it's crazy enough to make sense. The icicle will be well-hidden in the flask and it will also stay frozen in there. Once removed, it can be used to stab the murder victim once before melting in the steam. The weapon hasn't disappeared, it's melted."

"I'm going to have a hard time proving that," the inspector muttered. "I guess I'll go question the suspect who brought in the flask."

(Answers) The Case of the Impossible Escape

I left Sherlock to think and I went to make us both a cup of tea. It had only been a few minutes before he called me back into the living room.

"Watson! I've figured it out, Watson!"

I hurried into the living room to hear Sherlock's solution to the puzzle.

"There are several moves the boy has to make before he can find his way to freedom. He must first move fast to grab the snake and throw it at the lion. This will distract the lion for long enough so the boy can climb down to the ground and grab the axe. He must then use the axe to kill the lion while it is still distracted. He must then feed the lion to the crocodiles so he can escape without them following him."

Sherlock smiled at me, proud of himself for figuring it out.

"Well done, Sherlock. I couldn't figure it out myself, but I'm not surprised that you did." I told him. "Let's hope you aren't too bored now."

"I'm still bored and I still require more mental exercises."

"I'm making you a cup of tea, will that help?"

He thought for a moment and then nodded in response.

(Answers) The Case of the Man who Cheated Death

"It seems like a difficult puzzle but the answer is simpler than I originally thought," Sherlock finally said.

"Yes, I came to the same conclusion. Do you have the answer?"

"Death never returned because as soon as he left, the youngest son must have blown out the candle. He asked Death to let his father live until the wick of the candle was completely burned out, not the flame itself. Therefore, if he blows out the candle, the wick will never burn out and Death will never be able to return for the man's soul."

"I can't believe you solved it so quickly," I grunted, "It took me a good few hours."

"That's why you should opt for some quiet time after your walk rather than sitting here and reading books. Especially simple riddle books, like this one."

(Answers) The Case of the Crazed Kidnapper's Code

I eventually found the next number in the pattern once I realized what the pattern was. Each number in the sequence was a visual representation of the number before it.

The first number was 1 and so the next number was 11. It's basically telling us that there was one 1 in the previous number. The third number was 21, which is basically saying that the number before it had two 1's, and so on. Once I found this out it was easy to find the next number in the pattern.

The last number on the paper was 312211 and so the last number is a visual representation of that number. The last number in the sequence was 13112221. This means that there was one 3, one 1, two 2's, and one 1 in the number before it. Therefore, the full code for the lock was 1, 11, 21, 1211, 111221, 312211, 13112221. This is the code that Sherlock used to escape his cell and his kidnapper.

I finally figured it out, which made Sherlock upset that he was no longer the only one who could solve the puzzle. The inspector was still impressed that Sherlock managed to rescue himself from a kidnapper no matter how he did it.

(Answers) The Case of the Lost Survivalist

"I don't understand, Sherlock," I said when I heard the news. "Your friend had found a cabin. He was going to light a fire and stay there until his rescue arrived. How could he have died?"

"He froze to death, Watson, because he couldn't light a fire." Sherlock explained. "He mentioned earlier in the phone call that he had fallen into a river. Not only did he lose his map but he also soaked his clothes and all of his supplies. That includes the matches in his pocket that he was going to use to start a fire. Once matches get wet, they cannot be lit, even if they are completely dry. He couldn't start a fire, it was cold in the mountains, and his clothes were wet: These were the perfect conditions for him to freeze to death overnight."

"I can't believe it," I gasped. "I'm sorry you lost your friend, Sherlock."

I left Sherlock alone after that, because I knew that's what he needed.

(Answers) The Case of the Copycat Killer

I studied all the copycat killers carefully and in the end it was obvious which one was real and which ones were fake.

"How do you know he is the real killer?" The inspector asked me.

"He is more confident than the others," I explained. "The seven are copying him and so they kept glancing at him for confirmation that they were acting correctly. However, he was standing straight and he was confident. He didn't need to glance at the others for confirmation that he is acting correctly, because he is being himself."

"Brilliant!" Sherlock cheered. "Excellent way to think outside of the box, Watson. I don't think I would have come to the same conclusion in the same way. I would have come to the correct conclusion eventually, of course, just not using those exact methods. Watson is indeed correct, Inspector. That is your real killer and the rest are mere copycats."

(Answers) The Case of the Sudden Second Funeral

"The girl was infatuated with me," Sherlock explained. "She was obviously obsessed and she would do anything to get the chance to see me again. Since our first meeting was at a funeral, it makes sense that she would kill her father in order to arrange another funeral. She knows I am a friend of the family and that I would attend the funeral."

"That is a leap, Sherlock." I told him. "He is only missing, presumed dead. What if he is still alive?"

"Not likely, she is already arranging a funeral for her father even though he has been missing for only a few days. Something tells me she already knows that he is dead."

"I'll call Scotland Yard and let them know that she should be investigated," I told him and headed for the phone.

(Answers) The Case of the Day in Court

During the lawyer's final statement, he mentioned how the father of the young woman was only missing and could walk through the door at any moment. Everyone in the courtroom looked to the door and waited for the man to walk in - everyone except Sherlock and the young woman.

"This woman is guilty," Sherlock stated to the jury. "She already knows that her father is dead and that is why she didn't look at the door along with the rest of the courtroom. She didn't look at the door with the rest of the courtroom because she knew that her father would not walk through it and that is evidence that she is guilty in his murder."

The courtroom erupted in whispers and murmurs and the judge had to bang his gavel down to silence everyone.

"I say that she murdered her father and hid the body so it would look like he was missing. She then waited a few days before arranging a funeral and inviting me to it. She did this all so she could see me because she is obsessed with me."

When Sherlock had finished his statement, the jury released their verdict. They convicted her of all her crimes and she was sent to prison for the murder of her father.

(Answers) The Case of the Untouched Vehicle

"I thought you said it was a challenging case, Inspector?" Sherlock teased. "It's actually quite simple, and you gave the answer away at the beginning of your story."

"Oh did I? Come on then, Mr. Holmes, how was the man shot?"

"You mentioned that the car was a convertible at the beginning of your story. If the windows were rolled up and the doors were locked but the victim was shot from the outside of the vehicle, then it is safe to assume that the roof of the car was rolled down. Am I correct?"

I looked to the inspector and he wore an expression that was a mix between disappointed, stunned, and angry.

"Yes, Mr. Holmes, you are correct again. I just don't understand how you do it."

"It's elementary my friend. Simple elementary."

(Answers) The Case of the Murdered Chemist

"The names of the murderers are hidden on this note," Sherlock explained to the inspector. "Only a chemist or someone taught by a chemist would be able to decipher the code my friend left for me." Sherlock showed the note to me and the inspector and pointed to the collection of numbers. "These numbers correspond to the atomic numbers of certain elements on the periodic table. The first set of numbers, 26, 3, and 58, can be translated into the name, Felice. The second set of numbers, 28, 27, 57, and 16, can be translated into the name Nicolas. The murderers are Nicolas and Felice."

"Thank you for your help, Mr. Holmes, and I'm sorry for your loss." The inspector said. "We'll track these guys down and make sure they're punished for their crimes."

"Thank you very much, Inspector."

(Answers) The Case of the Captain's Missing Ring

"How can you be certain it was the seaman who took my ring?" The captain asked.

"It's simple, because his alibi is the only one that doesn't make sense." Sherlock explained. "He said he was correcting the flag because it was upside down, but you are a Japanese cargo ship and you sail underneath the Japanese flag. It looks the same no matter which way it is turned."

"I would never have guessed!" The captain's eyes were wide with surprise. "Thank you for your help, detective Holmes. Without you, I would never have found my ring and there would still be a thief aboard my ship. I'll have the police down here at once before I set sail."

"It was a pleasure, Captain." Sherlock bowed his head slightly.

We stayed for a while to see the ship off and the Captain waved to us from the front of it as they sailed out to sea.

Printed in Great Britain
by Amazon

15068698R00099